Mother Nature

A book about the journey of motherhood

Nicole Loudin

BookLeaf
Publishing

India | USA | UK

Dedication

To my dearest Kai, my adventurous, clever, and funny little boy. Every effort I make is for you. Since the moment you entered my life, you have transformed my world. I am profoundly thankful to be your momma. I love you dearly, my son.

Preface

Welcome to a little piece of my journey into motherhood!
This collection of poems is all about the wild and adventurous journey I've been on with my son. Since that first moment I held him, my life has never been the same, and every giggle, tantrum, snuggle, and life's challenges has inspired these verses.

Writing these poems has been my way of capturing the crazy, beautiful chaos of raising a free-spirited boy. From sleepless nights to sweet little milestones, to the challenges of raising a boy alone, to my own growth as a person and mother. I've poured my heart into these pages, hoping to share the joys and challenges that come with being a mom.

So, whether you're a seasoned parent, a new mom, or just someone who enjoys a good read, I hope you find a piece of your own journey in my words. Thanks for joining me on this adventure of love, laughter and everything in between!

Acknowledgements

I would like to extend my heartfelt thanks to the following people who have made this journey possible:

To my son, Kai, for inspiring every word I write and for filling my life with unconditional love and pure joy.

To my mother, for always being there through the good and the bad. For teaching me how to be the mother I am today. Your unwavering support keeps me going.

To my friend, Carissa, for being my biggest support system through all the challenges of motherhood and my love life. For filling my life with pure friendship, laughter, and love.

To Sean, for teaching me how to appreciate the small things, to look at everyday as a new beginning, to have gratitude for those around you.

To me, for never allowing my heart to harden and my character to weaken despite the things I've been through. For always going above and beyond for my son and those in my village.

1. My Son

4:34am

Brought forth on a day of deep gratitude.

A love ignited within me, profound and new.

The world around me faded, time lost it's grip.

You're here.

In this moment, I embrace my journey as your mother.

2. Christmas Magic

I caught the sparkle in your eyes when you
spotted the elf at Grandma's house,
his little form perched high, almost hidden
in the twinkling lights,
draped in holiday cheer, with a grin that
could warm the coldest nights.
"Coconut" is what you named him.
You turned to me, your eyes shimmering
with the wonder of the season,
and exclaimed, "Mommy, it was the magic!"
In that fleeting moment, I felt a wave of
nostalgia wash over me,
as memories of my own childhood
Christmases unfolded like a cherished storybook.
Behind every enchanting moment- like the
scent of pine, the glow of candles,
and the soft sounds of carols drifting
through the air -
there were my parents, crafting the magic
with love and care.

They filled our home with traditions,
laughter, and dreams,
transforming ordinary days into

extraordinary memories.
I realized that now it was my turn to create
those same moments for you,
to weave a tapestry of joy and wonder in
your heart.

I promised myself that next December,
when the snowflakes dance
and the world is wrapped in a blanket
of white,
he would have his very own special elf, just
for him,
a little companion to spark his imagination,
just like my parents did for me.
Together, we would create our own version
of magic,
one filled with love, laughter, and the
twinkle of holiday lights,
ensuring the spirit of Christmas lives
on in our hearts forever.

3. Beneath the Mistletoe

His skin, warm as the heat from the
crackling fire.
His eyes, emerald like the evergreen trees.
His smile, infectious like the winter flu.
His touch, gentle and secure sends chills
like the cold bite of winter.
His voice, soothing like the gentle fall of the
first snow.
His scent, sweet and masculine clings to
the walls.
My heart longs to experience his love
once more.
I yearn for his body pressed close to mine.
His breath whispers softly against my ear.
I desire him.
I need him.
A forbidden Christmas love.
But
"Santa's coming in the morning!!"
A four-year old boy, with shining eyes
full of awe
and magic,
relies on me.
Wipe your tears.

The show must go on.
My heart shatters silently like children
dreaming, waiting for St.Nick's arrival.
Our paths will intertwine again.
Beneath the Mistletoe.

4. Boys will be boys

Boys will be boys.
Is what they often claim.
"Mommy, he yanked my hair!"
"Oh, he just likes you, go ahead, don't
feel shame."
Boys will be boys; their roughness
is expected.
Crying is for the weak; emotions should
be rejected.
"Daddy, look a babydoll!"
"No son, those are for girls."

But my son,
My boy,
Will be taught not to bully.
But to love
and to cry
and to feel everything inside.
To feel safe and secure
playing with barbies and
dolls.
To wear pink if he so pleases while
racing trucks in the back yard,
Dirt under his fingernails.

A heart of pure gold.
He cares about the world around him.
At only four years old.
Boys will be boys, you say.
But my boy,
Will be a man someday.

5. Nature's Bond

Walking barefoot on the earth,
Collecting stones,
And leaves,
And acorns,
Chasing fireflies at dusk,
Creating messy mud pies-
You are truly one with nature.

Beneath the vast, blue sky,
You run freely, your laughter ringing,
As you dance with butterflies,
And gentle breezes whisper sweet songs.
You marvel at the rustling trees,
Listening to their stories as they sway,
Each branch cradling birds that sing,
A symphony of life in every way.

You prefer the outdoors,
The feel of grass beneath your feet,
The thrill of discovering new wonders,
Over a screen's cold, artificial glow.
Every moment spent outside
Is a treasure, a gift from the earth
That feeds your curious spirit,

Filling your heart with joy and mirth.

It fills my heart with pride, knowing
You inherited this love from me.
In a world that rushes and spins,
You find peace in nature's embrace,
A beautiful bond we share,
As we explore this magical place.

6. The laundry can wait

I call my mom,
"How did you ever handle this chaos?"
I'm perpetually exhausted,
Always feeling hungry,
The house is in disarray,
Toys scattered like confetti,
And laundry towers looming,
Piling up to the ceiling.

I'm overwhelmed,
With a million thoughts racing,
Each task feels monumental,
And i can't shake this sense of failing.
There's so much to accomplish,
Yet the clock ticks mercilessly,
Days slip through my fingers,
Like grains of sand in an hourglass.

He begs me to play,
His eyes filled with hope,
But the dishes are towering,
And the socks need sorting-
A never-ending cycle of chores,
Pulling me in every direction.

I feel stretched thin,
Worn down by the weight of it all.

She replies softly,
"One day, you'll yearn for this time.
These moments are fleeting.
The laundry can wait,
And the dust will settle,
You're doing better than you know."

7. Peace & Quiet

I crave the quiet of
An empty home.
The floors,
The counters,
Free of clutter.
The scent of citrus and sage
Permeates the space.
Just a day or two of
Complete solitude.
"I'll be back soon Mommy!"
But the hours stretch on, lonely and long.
I start to hear echoes of "Mommy".
I miss the laughter,
The endless questions,
The "Mommy, look at this!"
The scrunch on his nose when he
acts goofy.
The warmth of his hugs
And the sweet "Mommy, I love you."
My time away was refreshing,
Yet I miss my little one.
Vacation will soon come to an end,
And the house will once again be
Brimming with love and delightful chaos.

8. Single Mother

In the quiet dawn, with sun's first light,
A single mom rises, ready for the fight.
With tiny hands tugging, and laughter
so bright,
She embraces her role, with love
and delight.

Through sleepless nights and long,
weary days,
She navigates storms in so many ways.
With crayons and toys, they create their
own plays,
Building castles of dreams, in a world
that sways.

Yet sometimes the weight feels heavy
and stark,
Balancing work, life, and a flame in
her heart.
But in every hug, in each giggle and spark,
She finds strength in love, a powerful arc.

For her little boy's smile is worth every tear,
A bond that grows stronger with each

passing year.
Though the road may be tough, her
purpose is clear,
In the struggles of motherhood, there's
nothing to fear.

Together they'll conquer, hand in hand
they'll stand,
A fierce little team, in a vast,
wondrous land.
With courage and hope, and
dreams unplanned,
She faces each challenge, a hero so grand.

9. A land of giggles

In a land of giggles, where silliness reigns,
Lives a little boy who dances in rain.
With a crown made of paper and socks
worn askew,
He twirls like a tornado, oh, what can't
he do?

With a whoopee cushion and a cheeky
grin wide,
He's a master at mischief, his mom's
greatest pride.
They leap off the couches, they bounce off
the walls,
In a world full of laughter, they answer
the calls.

With wiggly worm moves and a funny
hat on,
They're a duo of joy from dusk until dawn.
Spinning in circles, they fall with a laugh,
Creating their own silly, whimsical path.

From mud puddle splashes to hopscotch
and skips,

They're the kings and queens of their goofy
little trips.
With tickle fights roaring and pillow
forts grand,
Life's an adventure, hand in hand as
they stand.

So here's to the fun, to the laughs that
they share,
A little boy's goofiness, a wild ride to dare.
In their joyful chaos, there's magic to see,
Just a goofy mom and her silly little spree!

10. Afraid of the dark

In a cozy little room where shadows
softly loom,
There's a little boy who trembles in
the gloom.
With wide, scared eyes, he peeks from
his bed,
Whispers of monsters dance in his head.

"Mom! There's monsters in here!" he cries
out in fright,
As the shadows around him come alive in
the night.
He shivers and clutches his blanket
so tight,
Fearing the creatures that hide out of sight.

His mom, with a heart that mirrors his fear,
Looks into the shadows; something
stirs near.
She hugs him close, her voice a soft thread,
"If there are monsters lurking, I'll guard you,
my dear."

"They might look a bit spooky, with eyes

that glow bright,
But we'll face them together, we'll conquer
the night."
Her gaze scans the corners, the whispers
take flight,
In the dark, she feels something stirring,
not right.

They gather their courage, with hearts
beating loud,
Creating a fortress of pillows, so proud.
With giggles and whispers, they fight off
the fear,
For in their brave hearts, the monsters
draw near.

And so in that room, where shadows
once roamed,
Lives a little boy and his mom, both
at home.
With fear not defeated, but woven in love,
They embrace all the mysteries, like stars
up above.

11. I'll stay where you are

I watch my little boy, as he drifts into sleep.
At just four years old, he's had loss that
cuts deep,
Yet he clings to my heart, where love's light
we keep.

"Mommy," he says.
"I miss him,
Where did he go?
Is he coming back?"
I reply "Honey, I don't know."

I see the sadness behind his bright eyes,
As he battles the shadows, the whispers,
the sighs.
"Sweet boy," I murmur, pulling him near,
"The world can be heavy, but I'm
always right here."

His little hands tremble as he draws in
the night,
Cloudy pictures of longing, where
everything's right.
I wish I could take all his worries away,

And shield him from sorrow, let him
just play.

"Mommy, I promise, I won't go too far,
Even when it gets heavy, I'll stay where
you are."
His words pierce my heart, a mix of
sweet fear,
For I know the truth of the world he
can hear.

In our little house, where love should
be bright,
I hold my dear boy, through the long
lonesome night.
With all of my strength, I wrap him in love,
For together we'll face what the dark
dreams are made of.

And though I feel heavy with burdens
we bear,
I'll cherish each moment, every whisper
we share.
For in his brave heart, I find strength to
stand tall,
A bond forged in love, that conquers it all.

12. Brave

In a busy, bright park where the children
all play,
Stands a shy little boy gripping onto his
mother's leg.

"Mommy," he whispers, clutching her
tight,
"I wish I were brave, but this feels like
a fight.
When kids start to giggle, I want to
join in,
But my voice feels all wobbly; it just
won't begin."

His mommy looks down, with a smile and
a nod,
"I know how you feel; it can be quite hard.
Just take a deep breath and look all around,
You can join in the fun; there's joy to
be found!"

"Let's take it slow, watch the swings start
to soar,
You have a big heart, and it's okay

to explore.
I'll be right here to help you along,
You're stronger than you think; you can't
go wrong."

With a squeeze and a grin, he feels a
bit brave,
Together they'll face it, together
they'll wave.
For even when shy, he can laugh and
be free,
In the bright, happy park, with his mommy
by the tree.

13. A mother knows best

Rejecting the norms that dictate how
to learn,
She seeks a new path, where
curiosity burns.
With memories of learning in a
nurturing space,
She knows that through exploration,
together they'll race.

With a globe in her hands and a map on
the wall,
She envisions a journey, where together
they'll sprawl.
Through mountain-top hikes and the
ocean's embrace,
In forests and meadows, they find their
true place.

Each lesson a treasure, each moment
a grace,
As nature unfolds, their spirits interlace.
With empathy nurtured and compassion
as key,
She'll teach him the values of kindness

and glee.

Life skills will flourish in the warmth of
their home,
As they cook and create, together
they roam.
No rigid bell warnings, just laughter
and play,
As they wonder through history in their own
special way.

From bustling city streets to quiet
forest trails,
Every step tells a story, every breeze
shares a tale.
Family bonding, the heart of their quest,
In the warmth of togetherness, they'll learn
at their best.

Through travel and wonder, they'll uncover
the world,
In the tapestry of life, their love will
be swirled.
So she casts aside fears, with courage
and might,
Crafting a future that feels just right.

With joy as their compass, adventure
their guide,
In the heart of their home, they'll flourish
side by side.

14. Two single moms

In a world that's wild and
wonderfully bright,
Two single moms stroll, sharing laughs day
and night.
With their young boys in a tow, they embrace
every play,
Rolling through life in their own easy way.

Through muddy adventures and nature's
sweet call,
They soak up the moments, enjoying it all.
With witchy vibes floating, their
spirits unwind,
Underneath the stars, they share what
they find.

From bedtime stories filled with magic
and cheer,
They tackle the chaos, with hearts open
and clear.
With herbal tea brewing, they plan and
they dream,
Back and forth and chatting, just flowing like
a stream.

They swap tales of wins and the bumps in
the road,
In a bond made of laughter, they lighten
the load.
Through scraped knees and giggles,
they stand side by side,
Building a village, with love as their guide.

With lessons in kindness, respect, and
good fun,
They nurture their boys, helping each one.
So here's to their journey, the giggles
and sighs,
To the strength found in friendship, where
true comfort lies.

Together they flourish, through all that
life sends,
Two single moms thriving, forever
as friends.

15. Embrace the waves

In quiet moments, I take a breath,
A mom just trying to do my best.
Sharing lessons, taking my time,
Sorting through the messy and sublime.

My past creeps in, but that's okay,
I'm here to guide him day by day.
"Embrace the waves, let them roll," I say,
"It's okay to feel, in every way."

I teach him gentle ways to cope,
To name his feelings, to find his hope.
With each word, I find some peace,
His laughter helps my worries cease.

In our cozy space, we learn and grow,
Two hearts together, taking it slow.
Side by side, through the ups and downs,
As mother and son, we find our ground.

16. Growing up

In the morning light, I sit and think,
About how fast you've grown, it makes
me blink.
From a tiny baby, all soft and new,
To a lively boy, with a world to pursue.

You're not that toddler who needs my hand,
You're off on adventures, making your
own plans.
Your laughter fills the air, bright and bold,
Yet I can't help but feel a little old.

Soon you'll be a teen, with dreams in
your eyes,
Facing the world and reaching for
the skies.
I'll watch from the sidelines, a mix of pride
and fear,
Wishing for moments when you were
still near.

Every little memory, I hold close to
my heart,
From bedtime stories to crafts we

would start.
Now you're growing, finding your way,
And I cherish our talks at the end of
the day.

Though change is coming, and I know
it's right,
I'll miss those small moments that felt
so bright.
But I'm here cheering you on, with love that
won't fade,
A mother's heart, in every choice
you've made.

So here's to the journey, whatever it
may be,
To the man you'll become, your spirit wild
and free.
Though you're not my baby, just know this
is true-
You'll always be my joy, my heart, my view.

17. Tantrums

It's time to play but
A little boy's mood is about
to sway.
He builds with blocks, but they
tumble down,
And suddenly, he's wearing a frown.

His tiny face scrunches, his voice starts
to boom,
A storm of frustration fills the whole room.
"Why won't this work?!" he shouts
in distress,
His little heart racing, feeling the mess.

With arms crossed tight and a pout on
his lips,
He kicks at the carpet, a few little flips.
I watch from the sidelines, trying to see,
How to help him through this, just him
and me.

"Hey baby, it's cool," I say with a smile,
"Let's take a deep breath and hang for
a while.

It's okay to feel mad, to let it all out,
I'm right here with you, without any doubt."

So I sit down beside him, give him a hug,
He starts to relax, feeling the love snug.
We count to three, let the tension release,
And soon he's grinning, finding his peace.

With a giggle and wiggle, the
tantrum subsides,
He jumps back to play, his heart full
of pride.
For little moments like these, they come
and they go,
Just a part of growing, a little boy's flow.

18. A Mother, A Grandmother

I see my mom with my son, a truly
heartwarming sight.
Her laughter flows like a gentle tune,
As they play on the floor, beneath the
afternoon moon.

She shares the games from her own
childhood days,
With stories and lessons, in countless ways.
I notice the spark in her eyes as he grins,
A bond that feels endless, where their
joy begins.

She teaches him kindness, how to make
and create,
With each treasured moment, it's simply
first-rate.
Her hands, though aged, are steady
and sure,
Guiding him softly, with love that is pure.

I can't help but smile, my heart feels
so light,

As I watch this connection, it's lovely
and bright.
In every embrace and each gentle phrase,
I see a love story that beautifully sways.

There's wonder in witnessing this circle
of life,
A mother, a grandmother, through joy and
through strife.
In this quiet moment, I cherish the view,
As they weave their own tale, just me and
them two.

So here in this space, I soak in the scene,
Grateful for love that's both simple
and keen.
For my son and my mother, in their
warm embrace,
Reminding me of home, of comfort,
and grace.

19. Dinosaur Land

Where sunlight dances and shadows sway,
Lives a little boy with big dino dreams
at play.
With dinosaurs spread all over the floor,
He roars and he giggles, always
wanting more!

T-Rex is king, with a thunderous roar,
As they stomp through jungles, and
waterholes galore.
He builds mighty towers from blocks
stacked high,
Imagining adventures beneath the blue sky.

Triceratops munches on leafy green treats,
While Pterodactyls soar with their
flapping feats.
Brontosaurus splashes in a pretend stream,
As the boy laughs wildly, lost in his dream.

With arms open wide, he leads the parade,
Through prehistoric lands that he's
lovingly made.
Each roar and each stomp brings a smile to his face,

In his dino-filled world, he's found his
own place.

As the day winds down and the sun starts
to set,
He hugs his dino friends, with no hint
of regret.
For in his heart, where wild dreams reside,
That little boy and his dinosaurs will
always collide.

20. Big Brother

With memories swirling, a heart turned
to stone.
You were just a little one, full of light,
And now, in this stillness, I feel the
goodbyes bite.

From our laughter together, so bright and
so free,
We painted the world in colors of glee.
Your hugs felt like sunshine, your giggles
like song,
In the embrace of our family, where I felt
I belonged.

But now, as the shadows stretch long on
the wall,
I miss you, dear child; It feels like a fall.
The end of a chapter, a love that
has changed,
Yet my heart holds a space that cannot be
rearranged.

I think of our moments, the games that
we played,

The joy in our days, in our own little parade.
You were not just a child; you were a part of
my soul,
And losing your laughter has taken its toll.

Though paths have diverged and the future
feels gray,
Know that I cherish you, more than words
can say.
In my heart, you will linger, a sweet melody,
A bond that won't fade, forever with me.

So as time moves on, and life finds its way,
I'll hold onto memories, come what may.
For though we're apart, I'll carry you near,
In my heart, you will always be dear.

21. Epiphany

I rise alone in this space I call home.
My thirties whisper secrets soft and true,
An epiphany blooms, bright like
morning dew.

Through sleepless nights and days that
just drift,
I've held onto worries, forgotten my gift.
But today, I breath deep, let go of
the stress,
A quiet realization, it's time to progress.

It's time to explore the depths of my soul,
To reclaim my passions and make
myself whole.
With each step I take, I shed the old skin,
Embracing the woman, the strength
from within.

I'll wander through dreams, like paths in
the woods,
Rediscovering who I am, what I once
understood.
With courage as my compass, I'll chart

my own way,
Unearthing the magic in each passing day.

So here's to the future, where I stand tall
and free,
A mother, a woman, finally learning to be.
In this perfect moment, I finally see,
The love I hold for myself is setting me free.